SECRETS OF HALLOWEEN
You didn't know!

IVY NAKPODIA-EGBON

Copyright 2022 © Ivy Nakpodia-Egbon

All rights reserved.

No part of this book may be reproduced, or stored in a retrieval system, or transmitted in any form or by any means, electronic, mechanical, photocopying, recording, or otherwise, without express written permission of the publisher.

Dedication

To my son, Neil. You are my sunshine.

To all my spiritual children that I have had the privilege to teach over the years.

Acknowledgements

I would like to thank God for the gift of writing and the passion for children He has blessed me with. I also want to thank my husband, Benson, and my son, Neil, for their encouragement and support during this journey.

I appreciate my spiritual parents, Pastor and Pastor (Mrs) Makinde for their input in my spiritual walk and entrusting me with the Children's Department for over a decade.

I thank my friend, Taiwo Owonikoko, for exposing me to the dangers of Halloween.

This acknowledgement would be incomplete without mentioning my brother, Laolu Ogunrombi, who really encouraged me in this journey.

Finally, I would like to appreciate my Regional Pastor Mrs, Pastor (Mrs) Caroline Adebayo-Oke, for encouraging me to be an author several years ago.

Contents

DEDICATION	ii
ACKNOWLEDGEMENTS	iii
INTRODUCTION	1
CHAPTER 1: HALLOWEEN	2
CHAPTER 2: ORIGIN OF HALLOWEEN	8
CHAPTER 3: SYMBOLS OF HALLOWEEN	15
A. Pumpkins	*17*
B. Death Symbols	*20*
C. Halloween Sweets And Treats	*21*
D. Witches And Evil Spirits	*22*
E. Animal Symbols	*23*
F. Trick Or Treat	*24*
CHAPTER 4: DANGERS OF HALLOWEEN	27
CHAPTER 5: THE DEVIL'S AGENDA	36
A. Tv Shows / Movies	*37*
B. Music	*38*
C. Games	*39*
D. Rainbow	*40*
E. Sexual Education	*41*

CHAPTER 6: ALTERNATIVE TO HALLOWEEN	43
Why The Need For An Alternative?	44
What Is Hallelujah Night?	45
CONCLUSION	47
A. Flee	47
B. Share This Information With As Many As You Can	48
BIBLIOGRAPHY	49

Introduction

This book you're about to read will change your life forever. You're about to discover secret things you never knew about Halloween and this discovery will cause a shift in your involvement and those of your loved ones henceforth.

Chapter 1

Halloween

Holidays are a special time to come together with family and friends to share special moments and memories together. There are so many special holidays and celebrations in Ireland and in the world today such as St. Patrick's, Easter and Christmas. Some are celebrated locally. Some are celebrated nationally and others globally at different times of the year.

One of such holidays is Halloween, which is usually celebrated on the 31st of October in many places across the world. It is very popular in the United States of America, Canada, United Kingdom and Ireland. It happens to be one of the world's oldest holidays, as it started over 2000 years ago.

In Ireland, Halloween is a big deal. I daresay it is as big as Easter and Christmas. From early August, towards the end of summer and just before children resume school in September, shops start displaying costumes, skeletons, scary props, coffins, ghost costumes and all sorts of ghoulish stuff. There are loads of treats and sweets on sale, cupcakes with spiders on it, ghost-shaped sweets, pumpkin-shaped sweets and treats etc. Children love it and they get to go out trick or treating – that is, going around the neighbourhood asking people for sweets or people get tricked (pranked) if they don't get any treats. These children dress up as witches, demons and monsters, carve pumpkins and eat candy with demonic symbols on them. It's so much fun, isn't it?

The devil loves Halloween so much because he knows it's the one day that many people will turn their back on God and invite Satan into their homes. The late founder of the Church of Satan, Anton LaVey, once said: ***"I am glad that***

Christian parents let their children worship the devil at least one night out of the year."

2 Kings 21:6 (AMP) says, *"He made his son pass through the fire and burned him [as an offering to Molech]; he practiced witchcraft and divination and dealt with mediums and soothsayers. He did great evil in the sight of the Lord, provoking Him to anger."* The NIR version says: *"He sacrificed his own son in the fire to another god. He practiced all kinds of evil magic. He got messages from those who had died. He talked to the spirits of the dead. He did many things that were evil in the eyes of the Lord. Manasseh made the Lord very angry."*

Unknown to some Christians, this is what they have done, sacrificing their children to another god on the altar of evil. Even if it's just that one day of the year, it's no harmless fun; you are covenanting with the devil, sowing your seeds- your children to the devil! You are raising an altar to the devil and to the kingdom of darkness.

Many people, even believers, unknowingly covenant their children to the devil on the altar of Halloween. Unfortunately, ignorance is no defence! No wonder many of these children have a hard time knowing the Lord when they become independent and have the capacity to make independent life choices. Some get possessed by demons; some get inflicted by diseases that have no business coming on them and some get hunted by the spirit of death due to their partaking in the dangerous but unsuspecting activities of Halloween.

Covenants are powerful such that they follow generations after generations. The Books of Exodus and Deuteronomy talk about how the iniquity of the fathers will be visited on the children right up to the third and fourth generation; therefore, whatever you introduce to your children now will be introduced to their own children and their children's children.

"The Lord...visits the iniquity of the fathers on the children and the children's children, to the third and the fourth generation." (Exodus 34:6-7; Deuteronomy 5:8-10). However, if you do not want to be a partaker of this, there are many ways to make sure your celebration is more Christ-centred and Christ-inspired than anything else. We will look at this later in the book. But first, let's look at the origin of Halloween and how it came to be so widely celebrated.

REVIEW QUESTIONS

1. What does Anton LaVey say about Halloween?

   _____
   _____
   _____
   _____

2. Do you celebrate Halloween?

   _____
   _____
   _____
   _____

3. Give a reason for your answer above.

   _____
   _____
   _____
   _____

Chapter 2

Origin Of Halloween

Halloween was originally celebrated to honour Samhain (pronounced "SAH-win") – the Celtic god of death. It is a pagan celebration that originated from the Ancient Celts over 2000 years ago. The Celts were a collection of tribes in Central Europe, who later spread out to Ireland, the UK, France and Spain.

Halloween has its roots in ancient Celtic traditions, and these traditions include things like using human bones and blood in rituals. They are rooted in witchcraft and occult practices. The first thing you will notice about Halloween is that it's a holiday that celebrates death. The scary costumes, scary decorations and scary treats all point to death.

Today, many people still celebrate it by dressing up as ghosts and demons, walking around town collecting candy from strangers. This type of activity can put your children's lives in danger, as you do not know who they are getting treats from. The treats could be laced with drugs, and your children could be molested as they can be a way to lure them indoor and into private places. This could lead children down the path of occultism. This, we know, is clearly against God's plan for His children.

The Bible warns us not to participate in pagan practices, as seen in Deuteronomy 18:10–11: "There shall not be found among you anyone who makes his son or his daughter pass through the fire, one who uses divination, one who practices witchcraft, or one who interprets omens, or a sorcerer, or one who casts a spell, or a medium, or a spiritist, or one who calls up the dead."

Halloween was coined from All Hallows' Eve or All Saints' Eve. It's the night before All Saints'

Day (November 1), a holy day which honours all Christian saints and martyrs who have died. On the 13th of May, 609, the feast of All Saints' Day was first celebrated to dedicate the Pantheon in Rome by Pope Boniface IV. However, during the reign of Pope Gregory III (731-741 AD), he dedicated a chapel at Vatican City in Rome to honour all the saints, particularly on the 1st of November. That became the new date for All Saints' Day. Some believed the date was moved closer to the pagan festival to try and bring the pagans into the church.

In celebrating Halloween, the Celts believed that for one night the spirits of the dead were able to enter this world and roam about freely. Modern witches believe it is a time when the "veil between the dead and the living is thin." During this time, there is no barrier between the physical realm and the spiritual realm; ghosts of those who had died could walk around freely among the living. To ward off these evil spirits, people would dress up in costumes so they would not be recognised by these wandering spirits. This tradition continues today, with many people dressing up as witches or other scary creatures to ward off evil spirits on Halloween night, claiming that they are doing so to be seen as spirits; however, this practice is not biblical because it promotes fear instead of faith. How will dressing up as something scary scare off evil spirits if they are not birds of a feather?

Logically speaking, there's a reason why groups of people on special assignments put on uniforms. It's so that identification of one another can be achieved. Soldiers, for example, put on the same uniform. Police officers put on the same uniform. Students put on the same uniform. That way, a soldier can distinguish his fellow soldier from an enemy in the battlefield.

When you choose to dress like a ghost, you're affirming that you're ready to die. You are telling spirits that you are a follower and, as a result, are exposing yourself to untimely death. When you dress like a demon, you're telling demons that you are a fellow or follower and they can be friends with you. 2 Corinthians 6:14b says, *"What has light got to do with darkness?"*

It is noteworthy that spirits of loved ones do not come back to the earth on a certain day or on certain days for anything whatsoever. The only spirits that God permits on earth are angels and demons. Once a man dies, his spirit leaves the earth forever. Whereas God's angels are on the earth for various assignments like protection, conveying messages from God to man and running errands. Demons, on the other hand, are messengers of the devil to bring pain and cause chaos to humanity, including your life, your children and all that concerns you. But we serve a living God; therefore, they will not succeed in Jesus' name. 1 John 3:8 says, *"The one who practices sin is of the devil; for the devil has sinned from the beginning. The Son of God appeared for this purpose, to destroy the works of the devil."*

The idea behind Halloween is from the pit of hell to deceive men into opening their lives, homes and children to the devil. Beware! The modern version of Halloween is not one that neither glorifies God nor celebrates His creation, rather it is one that glorifies death and gives people a license to indulge in their sinful nature. It's also a time when the world of darkness comes out to play.

Halloween has become increasingly popular over the years, with its focus on celebrating death and evil spirits. This idea has been promoted by Satan himself to make people believe that he has power over death and evil spirits, but he doesn't.

1 Peter 5:11 (The Voice) is one of the several scriptures that talk about the fact that ALL power belongs to God. It says, *"For all power belongs to God, now and forever. Amen."* Matthew 28:18 and Psalm 62:11 also affirm this truth.

Hallelujah!

REVIEW QUESTIONS

1. What is the origin of Halloween?

   _____
   _____
   _____
   _____

2. What does Halloween promote?

   _____
   _____
   _____
   _____

3. Why do people wear uniforms?

   _____
   _____
   _____
   _____

Chapter 3

Symbols Of Halloween

Halloween isn't as fun and harmless now, is it? Lots of people don't realise that Halloween is full of symbols that represent different things in the world and in our culture today. Ghosts are associated with death and mortality; witches are associated with black magic and evil; pumpkins are associated with jack-o'-lantern; black cats are associated with bad luck. The list goes on and on,

Each of the more popular symbols of Halloween has its significance. Trust me they are not as innocent as they are made out to be. I want to encourage you to think about what these symbols mean to you as a Christian.

When you see skeletons or witches or black cats, what do they remind you of? Do they make you think about how much God loves us? Or do they make you think about death or black magic? I think it's important that Christians take time to see the pending danger that lies ahead when this celebration is played down to nothing other than harmless fun. It's important for Christians to know this, not only because Halloween is a pagan holiday, but also because many people don't know that there are other spiritual forces (like demons and witches) at work behind these symbols and indeed during that time of the year.

A symbol is defined as a thing that represents or stands for something else, especially a material object representing something abstract. With that in mind, let's have a look and see what these symbols really represent.

A. PUMPKINS

Pumpkins are thought to have originated from Central America thousands of years ago; however, there's no direct evidence proving this theory. They were used by Native Americans as a food source and for decorative purposes long before Europeans arrived in North America. Pumpkins are just as much a part of Halloween as trick-or-treating and costumes. They are used in many ways—to decorate homes and yards, to make pies and soups and even as decorations themselves.

For Halloween celebrations, pumpkins are carved into scary faces, a candle is placed inside and it's used as a decoration inside the house, on lawns and yards. This scarily carved face pumpkin is known as a Jack-O-lantern and was traditionally made from Turnips in Ireland, not Pumpkins. Pumpkins only became popular after the Celts moved to the US, where there was an abundance of Pumpkins.

A Jack-o'-lantern is one of the most popular symbols of Halloween. The name comes from the Irish Myth of Stingy Jack, a man who invited the devil to have a drink. Now, as you may know, nothing good came out of this story, but I will tell you anyway. Stingy Jack, as his name suggests, didn't want to pay for his drink, so he asked the devil to change into a coin so he could pay for the drinks. For some reason, the devil agreed and changed into a coin. However, instead of Stingy Jack to pay for their drinks, he picked up the coin and put it in his pocket which had a silver cross.

With the silver cross in Stingy Jack's pocket, the devil was then trapped as a coin and could not change back to his initial form. This was one of a few ways that Stingy Jack scammed the devil. Eventually, the two came to an agreement: that Stingy Jack would free the devil if he agreed not to bother him for a period and not claim his soul when he died. So, the devil agreed and was set free.

When Stingy Jack died, he was not allowed into heaven because of how he was. Also, the devil wouldn't let him into hell because of the deal they had. He, however, threw Stingy Jack a coal to light his way as he roamed the Earth. Jack placed the coal in a carved-out turnip and got the name Jack of the Lantern aka Jack O'Lantern. This story is a myth - a widely held but false belief or idea, which is not true.

The Bible tells us that when we die, we go to heaven or hell. In other words, there are no other options. It also tells us that heaven is a place full of light and happiness; hell is a place full of darkness and despair. You can't roam the Earth aimlessly, so make sure you are heading in the right direction. If you have believed in Jesus, then you have the gift of eternal life; however if you haven't, there is an opportunity for you to do so now.

Say this prayer with the whole of your heart:

"O Lord God, I believe with all my heart in Jesus Christ, Son of the living God. I believe He

died for me and God raised Him from the dead. I believe He's alive today. I confess with my mouth that Jesus Christ is the Lord of my life from this day. Through Him and in His Name, I have eternal life; I'm born again. Thank you, Lord for saving my soul. I'm now a child of God."

B. DEATH SYMBOLS

These next symbols all represent death. Examples are ghosts, graveyards and skeletons. Each of these symbols reminds one of death. Remember, one of the beliefs from Samhain is that the ghost of loved ones roams the streets because the veil between the living and the dead is very thin during the festival.

The latter part of John 10:10 stresses that God has given life and has given it to us more abundantly. We are also reminded that in Him we live and move and have our being. Jesus is the way, the truth and the life. As a child of God, you have the life of God in you. You have Zoe! Jesus conquered death. He rose after the third day, so we have no business whatsoever with death.

Death is synonymous with darkness, while life is synonymous with light. 2 Corinthians 6:14 also asks what business light has with darkness. When we celebrate death or give it more importance than life, we are buying into the idea that Satan should be worshiped instead of God.

C. HALLOWEEN SWEETS AND TREATS

Another symbol of Halloween is sweets, chocolates, candy etc. This can symbolise temptation. It's like something enticing, alluring or something sweet that tempts us to sin (yes, sin can be sweet at the time you are involved in it). However, the aftermath is not so palatable; they can leave a very sour taste on the tongue. Evil spirits (demons) always try to trick us into doing bad things so they can get us in trouble with God. While sin (sweets, chocolates etc) is measurable when doing it, it will eventually cause enmity with God and bring destruction. Halloween treats are usually wrapped in spiders, skeletons and pumpkin designed wraps.

D. WITCHES AND EVIL SPIRITS

One of the most popular costumes for Halloween is witches. These are usually ugly old women with a pointy nose, pointy hat, a cat or a broom as an accessory. Witches are now more refined and are your regular everyday people, just the same way the devil is not as obvious with his horns and pitchfork anymore.

Witchcraft has been so modernised that it is widely accepted as a religion or should I say a cult. I am sure we have all heard the term "good witch" or some will say they do not use their witchcraft for evil but for good etc. However, over the years, I have been unable to find any positive definition of the word "witch." The Bible also does not regard witchcraft and sorcery in a positive light.

E. ANIMAL SYMBOLS

These include bats, black cats, owls and spiders. All these animals have one thing in common: they are all associated with evil or bad omens. Black cats have always been the witch's companion and they will often disguise themselves as a black cat or an owl. Bats and spiders can always be found at a haunted house. Bats are often associated with vampires because they are blood-sucking animals. They sleep during the day and only come out at night to play.

F. TRICK OR TREAT

This is not really a symbol, more like a habit/tradition or something synonymous with Halloween. This started out when people started leaving out food for the ghosts of dead loved ones passing by. The poor in the community then saw this as an opportunity, started dressing up as ghosts and were going about begging for food from home to home. Now, children dress up as ghosts, witches or something scary to go around collecting sweets – treats. The trick part is when you go to a house, ask for a treat and if you don't get one, you play a dirty trick on them.

These can include egging – when you throw raw eggs, usually at the windows of the house or car parked outside.

REVIEW QUESTIONS

1. Name 3 symbols of Halloween and what they mean.

   a) _____
   _____
   _____
   _____

   b) _____
   _____
   _____
   _____

   c) _____
   _____
   _____
   _____

2. Describe how these symbols make you feel.

　　_____
　　_____
　　_____
　　_____
　　_____

3. Give a reason for your answer above.

　　_____
　　_____
　　_____
　　_____
　　_____

Chapter 4

Dangers Of Halloween

The effect that Halloween has on children is not to be taken lightly. Statistically, around the 31st of October, there is an unusually high spike in crimes such as kidnapping, murder, accidents etc. There are more anti-social behaviours as a whole lot of costume parties and scary events are taking place across the world.

The devil is cunning. Ephesians 6:11 makes us aware that he has strategies. He doesn't just come at us with a pitchfork, fangs and horns; neither is he dressed in red and black. No. If he did, we would recognise him right away. So, he looks at ways in which he can infiltrate our space without being noticed. He is way more sophisticated and very subtle in his attacks. Trust me, the devil has so much more planned than we give him credit for. He has his army, known as demons, who are ready to do his work. He sends them on assignments: to be principalities and powers over different territories and get them to carry out his dirty work.

I am not trying to scare you but to enlighten you and make you aware of the tricks of the devil. He is not just a serpent that tempted Eve in the Garden of Eden in Genesis, the Old Testament of the Bible. He is still in business today.

Satan is in our schools, teaching the children they can be who they want to be because they feel a certain way. He says they can be male even if they were born female or vice versa. He's also teaching them that they can also choose to identify as non-binary.

Wikipedia defines non-binary as an umbrella term for gender identities that are not solely male or female. I heard a story recently of how a

Christian young lady was asked why she refused to refer to her classmate as their pronoun of choice. She asked the principal whether the school would agree that she be addressed as a Caucasian when she was obviously black. He responded in the negative. Further, she claimed that since that was the case, she should not refer to a boy as a girl and vice versa.

We need to teach our children how to stand up for themselves, for what they believe and for their faith in God. A child who is sure of their identity in Christ will not be confused as to whom they are or whose they are. 1 Peter 2:9 says, ***"But you are a chosen people, a royal priesthood, a holy nation, God's special possession, that you may declare the praises of him who called you out of darkness into his wonderful light."*** The Bible says that God created man and woman, Adam and Eve, not a non-binary entity. The actual definition of the word non-binary "is not relating to, composed of, or involving just two things." It is not composed of or involving the two things that

God ordained from the beginning of time, which was a man and a woman. Rather, they chose to violate God's order.

To choose to be neither or both or an extra entity is the ploy of the enemy. This is one of his schemes to destroy the identity of our children, to confuse their minds, to make them question themselves and ultimately seek answers outside the will of God. That is just one of the schemes the devil uses to get to our seeds, our children and our future generation.

However, Genesis 3:15 says, ***"our seeds will bruise the head of the serpent."*** This means that our children have a part to play in defeating the devil. We all do. We need to cover our children in prayer and arm them with the Word of God so that they can also be ready to fight this battle.

Let's say a prayer over our children for a few minutes:

"Lord, we place our children in Your hands. Teach them to love You and You alone. Let

them know who and whose they are. Help them to be confident in their identity as a child of God. Please protect their hearts and minds from the schemes of the evil one so that he will not get through with his evil thoughts and desires. Father, keep them safe from evil friends who have been assigned to pull them down into a life of sin. We cover them with the blood of Jesus. We proclaim and declare that our seeds will bruise the head of the serpent in the mighty name of Jesus. Amen!"

Given the dangers of Halloween, the devil's plan is for us to underestimate his plans and devices, and he is very subtle in his manner of approach and delivery. His plan is to take as many children as possible into the occult unknown to them and to their parents.

So why does this matter? It matters because when we celebrate Halloween, we're celebrating something God hates: evil (Romans 6:23). We should be celebrating something God loves: life.

Children are exposed to all sorts during Halloween. While out tricking or treating, they can be molested, kidnapped or they can be given sweets or treats that can initiate them into witchcraft. Some have been involved in vandalism and bonfire just because their friends asked them to. Others have lost their lives in freak accidents from dare that they took part in. This could be in person or virtually as we have seen a lot of deaths arising from dares from various social media platforms such as the Blackout Challenge or the deadly Red Door and Yellow Door.

Car accidents always spike up in the week of Halloween compared to other weeks in October. A few things account for this, like drunk drivers leaving parties intoxicated and then choosing to drive in that condition.

Children who are mostly dressed in dark costumes cannot be easily seen usually on dark roads. They are so excited to be out tricking or treating that they forget about the safety rules they have been taught about crossing the road.

REVIEW QUESTIONS

1. Name 3 dangers of Halloween

a) _____
   _____
   _____
   _____

b) _____
   _____
   _____
   _____

c) _____
   _____
   _____
   _____

2. How can we guard our minds?

   _____
   _____
   _____

3. On what/whom do you base your identity?

   _____
   _____
   _____
   _____

Chapter 5

The Devil's Agenda

The devil is really raging and is coming up with different schemes every day. There are two ways that Satan gets into our minds: our eyes and ears. Both of them are gateways for evil spirits to enter our minds and hearts. So, be sure that you're keeping these areas guarded against temptations. We need to be careful what we allow into our space, what we watch and what we listen to. I have come to understand that media is the only thing that gains access into our minds without permission. Likewise, the easy access of children and the youth to the internet poses a danger to them.

A. TV SHOWS / MOVIES

Every TV show and movie now has an aspect of the LGBT agenda; it's known as being inclusive. The sad part is that this includes children's TV shows. Christians should choose what they want their children exposed to and how they choose to do that should be entirely up to them. They need to rise to the challenge and take over territories, especially in the 7 mountains of influence: **family, religion, education, media, arts and entertainment, business and government**. Media and arts and entertainment are being attacked massively by the devil. We need more Christian content, movies, TV, music etc. more than ever before.

The Craft, a movie, changed Jenny Weaver's life. It made her want to be a witch so much that she became one. She was delivered from that world because God had her in mind and had a plan and purpose for her life. She left witchcraft behind because she literally scared herself with her power and the things she could do.

In her testimony, she recalled stretching out her hands towards a chest of drawers and pulling it out without being touched. She could hear demons, feel and see things that the eye couldn't see. Today, she is an advocate for Jesus, telling the whole world about the plans of the evil one and how to be delivered from a life of witchcraft and demons.

B. MUSIC

There are new styles/genres that are just downright demonic. The videos are so graphic with sexual connotations, religious mockery etc. This is one of the devil's strongest agenda. The devil has been linked with the ministry of music, as recorded in Ezekiel 28:13: ***"You were in Eden, the garden of God; every precious stone was your covering: The sardius, topaz, and diamond, Beryl, onyx, and jasper, Sapphire,*** *turquoise, and emerald with gold. The workmanship of your timbrels and pipes was prepared for you on the day you were created.* "An Israeli psychologist, Naomi Ziv, concluded that "music can make people more compliant, more aggressive and even racist." Such is the effect music has on people.

C. GAMES

The gaming world is another means being used by the devil to further his wicked and evil agenda. Some games are violent, while some are just downright demonic and occult. It makes you wonder whether they are really for kids. Children and youths have easier access to games now through the internet, especially on their phones. Therefore, parents need to be mindful of the kind of games they allow their children to play. The Cult of the Lamb seems to me a game for introducing people to the world of the occult.

D. RAINBOW

The rainbow is a symbol of God's promise never to destroy the world. Genesis 9:13 says, ***"I have placed my rainbow in the clouds. It is the sign of my covenant with you and with all the earth."*** However, it has been hijacked by the LGBTIQ. It is now a symbol of inclusivity rather than a reminder of God's great love for us. I love bright colours and would love to wear shoes, bags and other accessories. But I keep thinking if I do, I will be thought of as a supporter of the movement. So, I tend to stay away from anything with a rainbow style print or design.

E. SEXUAL EDUCATION

This subject is now being used as an excuse to teach children all manners of things that a child has no business knowing. They are being taught about their sexual orientation and their rights to be who or what they want to be. From as little as age 4, there are books on same sex marriages to show the different family types, books on why it's normal to like a boy if you are a boy etc. .

I don't know about you, but I don't want my 4-year-old to be taught about issues like this at such a young age. I will teach them what they ought to know at the right time. I advise that you check the school curriculum of wherever you reside and make sure you know what your kids are being taught.

REVIEW QUESTIONS

1. Which of the devil's agenda is more prevalent in your children's school?

   _____
   _____
   _____
   _____

2. How can you fight these agenda?

   _____
   _____
   _____
   _____

3. Do you know what the school curriculum cover's regarding Sexual Education in your child's school?

   _____
   _____
   _____

Chapter 6

Alternative To Halloween

Having read about the origin, symbols and the dangers of Halloween, you have now been enlightened about the agenda of the devil for children through this holiday. That said, the good news about this is that there are alternatives to Halloween that you can celebrate.

WHY THE NEED FOR AN ALTERNATIVE?

We need an alternative to Halloween to counteract the forces of the evil operating at that time of the year. We need to spread the good news of Jesus, His love, peace, and faith, not fear. I was introduced to the term "Hallelujah Night" by a friend a long time ago.

She was my Head of Department in the children's church where I was volunteering as a teacher. We would have an Hallelujah Night celebration instead of Halloween and Taiwo, my friend, would teach an object lesson on how we should shine our light as children of God and not be a part of the darkness the world was entertaining at that time. Eventually, after I took over the children's church a few years later, I really started researching and looking at diverse ways in which we could celebrate HALLELUJAH NIGHT.

WHAT IS HALLELUJAH NIGHT?

The Urban Dictionary defines HALLELUJAH NIGHT as a fundamentalist Christian "anti-Halloween" celebration that takes place on the 31st of October.

The concept of Hallelujah Night is to shift the children's focus off all the evil going on around them which causes fear. They are encouraged to focus on Jesus who is the author and finisher of their Faith. They should place their faith over fear. The idea is to do something fun for the children while still honouring God during this time of year.

There are several ways we can celebrate Hallelujah Night or Day, depending on whatever time that suits you. You can have a fun day with the children in your church or neighbourhood. I usually have one for the children's department in my church where children are taught why we do not celebrate Halloween and what they can do to reinforce the biblical truths taught about the dangers of Halloween.

You can use an object lesson to drive home the point. For example, did you know that pumpkins can also be used as a symbol for something else? It can represent the way we should shine our light in this dark world, like Christ did here on earth by showing people love through His life, death and resurrection.

Get a pumpkin, cut the top off and start scooping out the seeds and pulp. **As you do this, talk about how you need to get rid of all your sins, evil ways and prepare your heart so that Jesus can come in and shine His light in your life.**

Carve out a cross, get a candle, light it and place it inside the cleaned-out pumpkin. **Explain to the children to shine their light for all to see**. If you choose not to go with pumpkins, there are plenty of other symbols that you can use.

Conclusion

I'm so glad you read to this point. Now that you have all these information, what should you do?

A. FLEE

Stay away from this celebration and anything that encourages it. The Bible tells us in 1 Thessalonians 5:22: *"Stay away from every kind of evil."*

B. SHARE THIS INFORMATION WITH AS MANY AS YOU CAN

Knowledge is power. We perish from the lack of knowledge. Daniel 12:3 says, *"Those who are wise will shine as bright as the sky, and those who lead many to righteousness will shine like the stars forever."*

Be a part of the movement who wants to bring down the works of the devil. Remember, Ephesians 5:11 says, *"Take no part in the unfruitful works of darkness, but instead expose them."*

Cheers to the new you!

Bibliography

https://www.easyvoyage.co.uk/travel-deal/the-top-10-ways-to-celebrate-halloween-/dublin-parade

https://www.unitedlanguagegroup.com/blog/translation/how-halloween-is-celebrated-around-the-world

https://www.history.;com/news/history-of-the-jack-o0lantern-irish-origins

https://wwwzodiacsigns101.com/symbolism/halloween-symbols/

https://www.whas-your-sign.com/meaning-of-halloween-symbola.html#google_vignette

https://www.worldpopulationreview.com/country-rankings/countries-that-celebrate-halloween

www.ingramcontent.com/pod-product-compliance
Lightning Source LLC
Chambersburg PA
CBHW050312220526
45465CB00005B/1952